Contents

CLASSIC FESTIVAL SOLOS, Volume 2 is a counterpart to the companion, Volume 1. Idiomatic solo materials with an eye to variety and playability are included, beginning with easier material and progressing to more difficult.

Works from several periods of composition are presented to give the advancing student the opportunity to learn and to demonstrate performance in each appropriate style. Technical progression is taken into consideration as well as program appeal for both soloist and audience.

Jack Lamb, Editor

NOCTURNE

CHARLES FORSBERG
Edited by MILES JOHNSON

CANTERBURY ROUND

CHARLES FORSBERG
Edited by MILES JOHNSON

EL03889

MELODY FOR JANE

F. WEBER

ON WINGS OF SONG

EL03889

SIMPLE GIFTS

TRADITIONAL
Edited by MILES JOHNSON
Arranged by CHARLES FORSBERG

BOURÈE

Edited by MILES JOHNSON
Arranged by CHARLES FORSBERG

Copyright © 1991 BELWIN MILLS PUBLISHING CORP., c/o CPP/BELWIN, INC., Miami, FL 33014
International Copyright Secured   Made in U.S.A.   All Rights Reserved

MARCH IN B♭

CHARLES FORSBERG
Edited by MILES JOHNSON

Themes from

ACADEMIC FESTIVAL OVERTURE

JOHANNES BRAHMS
Arranged by JAMES D. PLOYHAR

Copyright © 1970 BELWIN MILLS PUBLISHING CORP., c/o CPP/BELWIN, INC., Miami, FL 33014
International Copyright Secured   Made in U.S.A.   All Rights Reserved

TO SPRING

EDVARD GRIEG
Edited by PHILIP FARKAS
Arranged by LEONARD B. SMITH

One of Grieg's finest melodies. Try to imagine how a great string orchestra might sound in the original version. Play it softly but with an exceptionally round and mellow tone. In spite of the many notes which are tongued, they must absolutely touch each other so that there is no space between them except where the natural phrasing would require one to breathe. In the **12th bar**, where the music is marked pianissimo, play as softly and in as hushed a manner as possible. Then the crescendo molto starting **15 measures from the end** will be a thrilling, great exhalation of sound, all the more effective because of the previous beautiful pianissimo. *P. F.*

ROMANZE
Op. 138, No. 5

ROBERT SCHUMANN
Edited by MILES JOHNSON
Arranged by CHARLES FORSBERG

*Trill is optional.

RUSSIAN DANCE

C. KOPPRASCH
From Study No. 45
Arranged by REID POOLE

EL03889

FANTASIE

FR. STRAUSS
Edited by MAX. P. POTTAG

SARABANDE

JOHANNES BRAHMS
Arranged by REID POOLE

Slowly, but with steady rhythmic pulse
with full tone and sustained melodic line